S0-BBN-777

DISCARDED

RABBITS

Jen Green

Grolier
an imprint of
SCHOLASTIC

www.scholastic.com/librarypublishing

Published 2008 by Grolier
An imprint of Scholastic Library Publishing
Old Sherman Turnpike, Danbury,
Connecticut 06816

For The Brown Reference Group plc
Project Editor: Jolyon Goddard
Copy-editors: Lisa Hughes, Tom Jackson
Picture Researcher: Clare Newman
Designers: Jeni Child, Lynne Ross, Sarah Williams
Managing Editor: Bridget Giles

Volume ISBN-13: 978-0-7172-6280-9
Volume ISBN-10: 0-7172-6280-4

Library of Congress Cataloging-in-Publication Data

Nature's children. Set 3.
p. cm.
Includes bibliographical references and index.
ISBN 13: 978-0-7172-8082-7
ISBN 10: 0-7172-8082-9
1. Animals--Encyclopedias, Juvenile. I. Grolier Educational (Firm)
QL49.N384 2008
590.3--dc22
2007031568

Printed and bound in China

PICTURE CREDITS

Front Cover: **Nature PL**: Pete Cairns.

Back Cover: **Alamy**: fbkmedia.de, Pet Stock Boys; **Photolibrary.com**: Diaphor La Phototheque; **Shutterstock**: Charles F. McCarthy.

FLPA: Mitsuaki Iwago 10, S., D., K, Maslowski 29, Cyril Ruoso/JH Editorial 21, Roger Tidman 33, Duncan Usher/Foto Natura 46; **Nature PL**: Hermann Brehm 6, David Kjaer 17, Reinhard/Arco 42, Shattil and Rozinski 34; **NHPA**: Ernie Jones 14, Manfred Manegger 22; **Photolibrary.com**: Robert Lubeck 41, Thorsten Milse 37, Mike Powles 2–3, 18; **Shutterstock**: Copeg 9, Sharon D. 5, Larsek 4, 30; **Still Pictures**: G. Delpho/Wildlife 45, R. Linke 26–27, McPhoto 13, S. Meyers 38.

Contents

FACT FILE: Rabbits

Class	Mammals (Mammalia)
Order	Hare-shaped animals (Lagomorpha)
Family	Hare and rabbit family (Leporidae)
Genera	11 genera
Species	There are 62 species of rabbits and hares in the world
World distribution	Widely distributed except on the islands of southeast Asia and Antarctica; rabbits are now common in Australia
Habitat	Varied, from grasslands to woods, forests, mountains, deserts, and tundra
Distinctive physical characteristics	Long ears, compact, furry body, and white, fluffy tail; fur usually brownish, but some hares have white fur in winter
Habits	Active mainly at night; breed quickly, producing several litters in a year
Diet	Grass, buds, twigs, tree bark, and lichen

Introduction

Rabbits and hares live mostly in fields and woodlands. They are found almost everywhere in the world. Rabbits are well known for their plant-nibbling habits and for being capable of producing a lot of babies very rapidly. Hares have been famous for their speed since the Greek writer Aesop wrote the fable of "The Hare and the Tortoise." Rabbits are not very fast runners and are not able to sprint away from danger like hares can. Instead, rabbits dash into an underground network of burrows to escape danger.

A rabbit crouches in the grass.

Hares live out in the open. They are always listening and watching out for approaching danger.

Meet the Family

Rabbits and hares belong to a family of **mammals** called lagomorphs (LA-GUH-MORFZ). The word means "hare-like animal." Pikas are close cousins of hares and rabbits. They also belong to the lagomorph family. These furry mammals are smaller than their cousins. They have round ears and a tail, but the tail is not visible.

There are 62 **species**, or types, of rabbits and hares living around the world. The family's smallest member, the pygmy rabbit, weighs a little more than half a pound (0.3 kg). The largest species, the European hare, weighs up to 11 pounds (5 kg)—as much as 16 pygmy rabbits. The rarest species is the volcano rabbit. It lives only on the slopes of one mountain near the Mexican capital, Mexico City.

Rabbit or Hare?

The world of rabbits and hares can be confusing. The two groups of creatures are actually quite different. But they look so much alike that it is easy to get them mixed up. Some have even been named wrongly! For example, the Belgian hare is actually a rabbit, and the jackrabbit is a hare!

So how do you tell a rabbit from a hare? Rabbits are smaller, with a rounded body. Hares have longer ears and legs, and a leaner body shape. Newborn rabbits and hares are easy to tell apart. Baby rabbits are born blind, with no fur on their body. They are helpless for the first week of life. Baby hares are born with a furry body and open eyes. They are stronger and begin to hop around just a few hours after birth.

This jackrabbit has long ears and is, in fact, a hare.

Rabbits run wild in Australia, where they are now seen as pests.

Rabbit World

Rabbits and hares are right at home in most parts of the world. They live on every continent except the icy continent of Antarctica. However, there were no rabbits living in Australia until people brought them there in the nineteenth century.

Rabbits and hares can survive in all sorts of wild places, including grasslands, woods, and marshes. Some types thrive in harsh places, such as mountains, deserts, and the bleak, open tundra. Rabbits have even set up home in many city parks. If you live in the countryside or a small town, you might find that rabbits visit your garden—whether they are welcome or not!

Friend or Foe?

Rabbits and hares are generally likeable animals. They look cuddly and soft like a favorite stuffed toy. In western countries, rabbits are linked with Easter through the Easter bunny. In some countries, hares are thought to be magical creatures, while in China people used to believe a giant hare lived on the Moon.

However, rabbits and hares aren't popular with everyone. Many farmers and gardeners see them as pests, because they nibble tender plants. Rabbits caused a lot of problems in Australia after they were released there in the 1850s. They were meant to provide food for people and to be hunted for fun, but they bred so quickly that rabbits were everywhere by the 1900s! The rabbit population in Australia is now controlled very carefully.

A hare nibbles a farmer's lettuce crop.

This hare has made a form for itself in the snow.

Snug Hollow

Mammals, such as badgers, woodchucks, and foxes, dig cozy **burrows** to rest in—but not hares. These long-eared animals simply snooze in any sheltered nook they find. That might be a clump of grass, a hollow tree trunk, or under the overhanging branches of a tree. As the hare snuggles down, it creates a little hollow. This hare-shaped hollow is called a **form**.

Hares might use several forms, but they usually have a favorite nook that they consider home. In winter, hares take shelter in short tunnels that they scratch into the snow. Though made of snow these homes are surprisingly warm.

To Burrow or Not?

People in different parts of the world have different customs. So do hares and rabbits. In Europe, rabbits dig long burrows. They use them to sleep in and to hide from their enemies. Large numbers of rabbits live together in a network of burrows called a **warren**. Across the Atlantic Ocean, North American rabbits do not dig burrows. They rest in forms like hares instead.

No one knows why North American rabbits don't dig burrows like their European cousins. They will sometimes take over a burrow made by another animal—usually a skunk or woodchuck. But for the most part, they are happy to stay aboveground in their forms. However, one North American rabbit is an exception to the rule. The pygmy rabbit of the southwestern United States does dig its own burrow.

Two European rabbits crouch at the entrance to their burrow.

Something has distracted this family of European rabbits.

Sociable or Solitary?

Some rabbits and hares like company more than others. North American rabbits, jackrabbits, and snowshoe hares are loners. They meet up with others of their kind usually only to breed.

However, other species are more sociable. Arctic hares, northern snowshoes, and European rabbits live in large groups, which may contain more than a hundred animals. Parents, children, uncles, and aunts all share the same feeding site without quarreling. However, the animals often play-fight or chase one another in games of tag.

Some rabbits and hares are friendly to their own kind. However, the two groups of animals are not friendly toward each other. You will rarely see rabbits and hares together in the wild.

What's for Dinner?

Whatever their differences, hares and rabbits have one thing in common. They are all **herbivores**, or plant eaters. Rabbits and hares love fresh greens, and they don't care where they find them. It's no wonder farmers and gardeners view them as pests!

While rabbits mainly eat grass, they eat other types of plant food, too, such as twigs, buds, and tree bark. Hares that live in the Arctic region dig down through the snow to get at moss and lichen (LIE-KUN). In the struggle to survive the harsh winter, Arctic hares may even eat small animals and dead meat. They are the only type of rabbit or hare to eat any kind of meat.

A rabbit eats
wild violets.

A hare shows off its sharp teeth.

Born to Nibble

Rabbits and hares are well equipped to gather plant food. They have two large, sharp, chisel-shaped front teeth in their upper jaw. These teeth, called **incisors**, are perfect for nipping off the tops of plants. Strong back teeth, called **molars,** grind tough plants to a pulp.

If a rabbit's teeth got worn down, it would be unable to feed. Fortunately, the incisors keep growing throughout the animal's lifetime and, therefore, stay long and sharp. Mammals such as squirrels, rats, and mice also have incisors. But they lack the extra pair of small, sharp teeth just behind the incisors that hares and rabbits have. This second pair of cutting teeth is one of the main features that separates rabbits and hares from other gnawing animals.

Nighttime Activity

Rabbits and hares are mainly nocturnal. That means they are active at night. They spend most of the day resting in their forms or burrows. While resting they will often nibble at their fur to clean it. That is called grooming. As the Sun goes down they come out to find food. At night there are fewer **predators** about, so feeding is safer.

Mammals such as woodchucks, dormice, and ground squirrels don't stay active all year round. They survive the winter by entering a special deep sleep called **hibernation**. Hares and rabbits don't hibernate, but remain active all year. Even in the depths of winter, they are out and about, searching for food.

Hopping Aces

Hares and rabbits don't use their legs for walking, as dogs, cats, and humans do. Instead, they hop, using their powerful back legs like springboards. Hares and rabbits are amazing jumpers and sprinters. Snowshoe hares can leap about ten times their own length in a single bound. They can also jump 15 feet (4.5 m) straight up in the air. That puts human high-jump champions to shame!

Hares are also excellent sprinters. They can race along at nearly 50 miles (80 km) per hour over a short distance. At that speed, they can keep pace with the traffic speeding along highways! Rabbits can only run about half as fast as hares. But like hares, rabbits are very agile. They can quickly and easily change direction even when moving at top speed.

A hare runs at top speed through a meadow.

Swimming Rabbits

The hopping skills of hares and rabbits are well known. But did you know one type of rabbit is also good at swimming? The swamp rabbit, a type of cottontail, lives in marsh country in the southeastern United States. These rabbits love wet places. Their thick fur is waterproofed, which keeps their skin from getting wet. In summer swamp rabbits wallow in creeks and muddy pools to keep cool. As well as being an expert swimmer, the swamp rabbit is also a good diver! To escape its enemies on land, a swamp rabbit will dive headfirst into the water. It will then stay hidden underwater, poking only its nose above the surface to breathe. However, the swamp rabbit has to stay alert in the water, too, because alligators are also one of its enemies!

A swamp rabbit hides in a reed bed beside a marsh.

This eastern cottontail rabbit is the most common rabbit in North America.

On the Alert

The world is a dangerous place for hares and rabbits. Predators, such as owls and foxes, are always on the prowl for their next meal. Rabbits and hares must always be on the lookout for enemies—even while feeding.

Luckily, their long ears pick up every tiny sound. Hares and rabbits can swivel their ears to pinpoint the source of sounds. Also a great help is their finely-tuned nose, which picks up the faintest scent of predators. These timid creatures also sense the ground shaking as people or large animals pass by. If a predator approaches, the hare or rabbit crouches and stays completely still. It flattens its ears and body. In this position it no longer looks like an animal, but like a small rock!

Survival Skills

Many predators will pass right by a hare or rabbit crouching in the grass without noticing it. But if an enemy comes too close, and the rabbit feels threatened, it explodes into action. It leaps high in the air, then streaks away. The rabbit weaves to and fro in a zigzag pattern, which makes it difficult for any predator to catch.

The rabbit's bobbing tail acts as a white warning flag to other rabbits nearby. Once alerted, they will also run away. Hares and rabbits that live in groups may thump the ground with their feet to warn others of danger.

Rabbits and hares are usually quiet. But they can make a very loud squealing noise if they are captured. The ear-splitting noise can sometimes cause the predator to drop its victim. The rabbit can also kick out with its strong hind legs if captured. Any of these tactics may save a rabbit's skin!

Something has scared this rabbit and it is on the move.

Snowshoe hares have fur covering the soles of their feet to keep them warm when walking on snow.

Changing Color

The brownish fur of hares and rabbits helps them to hide in their surroundings. That is called camouflage. The hares of the far north do a more complicated disappearing act. Their fur changes color with the seasons, to match the changing landscape.

The varying hare is named after its changing fur. In winter its white coat camouflages the animal against the snow. In spring it sheds this coat and grows brown fur, which helps it to hide in the forest. This hare is also called the snowshoe hare, because its very long, furry hind legs act as snowshoes. They let the hare glide over thick snow without sinking through the crust.

Arctic Survivor

The Arctic hare lives even farther north than its cousin the snowshoe. It looks quite similar, but is almost three times larger. The extra weight helps the Arctic hare to keep warm, because a large body keeps its heat better than a small one. The Arctic hare has small ears, which often lie flat against its back. This helps protect the ears from getting frostbite.

To survive the bitter cold, the Arctic hare has a special fur coat made up of two layers. The long, silky hairs of its outer coat keep the moisture and wind out. The short, dense underfur keeps the animal nice and warm. When the icy wind blows, the hare sits facing into the wind. The wind then blows the hare's silky fur against its body, which helps keep its body heat from escaping.

This Arctic hare is completely white, apart from the black tips of its ears.

Male hares fight
to win a mate.

Time to Mate

Early spring is the start of the **mating season** for hares and rabbits. The babies will be born in late spring or summer, when the weather is warm and there is plenty of plant food around for them to eat.

When two males, called **bucks**, want the same mate, they may fight. The bucks dance around each other, then rear up on their hind legs and box with their front paws. "Mad as a March hare" is a saying that comes from this behavior. The winner courts the female by chasing her around in circles. The two also get to know each other by grooming each other's fur and leaping high in the air.

Baby Rabbits

About a month after mating, the **doe**, or female, rabbit gets ready for the birth. She prepares a nest in a burrow or a hollow in the ground. To make the nest cozy, she lines it with grass, moss, and fur plucked from her own coat. The nest is small—just big enough for the babies to fit inside.

The group of young born to the mother is called her **litter**. A doe can have three to six litters a year, with five or six babies each time. The female crouches above the nest, and gives birth to babies called **kits**. Newborn rabbits are tiny—just 3 inches (8 cm) long. They have no fur, cannot see, and are completely helpless. But they are born knowing how to seek and drink their mother's milk.

Baby eastern cottontail rabbits snuggle up in their nest.

Leverets huddle, waiting for their mother to return.

Hare Families

Hares have fewer litters than rabbits, and there are usually fewer babies each time. The mother-to-be does not prepare a nest for her young. Instead she just hides in a sheltered nook when it is time to give birth.

Baby hares are called **leverets**. They are about the size of chipmunks, and they are covered with fine fur. Leverets are born with their eyes open. They are on their feet just a few hours after birth. While leverets are less helpless than newborn rabbits they still need their mother to protect them. Like all baby mammals, they also drink milk from their mother.

Keeping Safe

Many female mammals stick close to their babies during their first weeks of life. Hares and rabbits do not. The mothers leave the babies alone for hours while they go off to feed. After covering the nest as best as she can, the female hops away. She only returns to feed her babies. However, she never strays too far from the nest. She feeds close by, and if a predator approaches, she takes flight in an effort to draw the enemy away.

Mother hares nurse their babies just once a day. The female creeps back to the nest when it is dark. That way, no predator learns where the young ones lie hidden in the grass.

The mother of this young rabbit has left it alone while she searches for food.

Two young rabbits nuzzle each other.

Growing Up

Young hares and rabbits grow up very quickly. In just three weeks the leverets are ready to leave the nest. Baby rabbits take a little longer to grow up—but not much! They leave home at five or six weeks. The young may stay together for a time. They will then split up and go their separate ways.

The young animals are a lot less wary than the adults. Many become the **prey** of predators, such as owls and foxes, before they reach full size. Those that do make it through the first weeks will soon be ready to find mates for themselves, and start a family. With luck, rabbits live for two years, and hares for three years, in the wild.

Nature's Balance

Hares and especially rabbits are famous for breeding quickly. In the course of a year, a single pair of rabbits can produce 80 offspring, who will produce 1,500 offspring of their own. That's an awful lot of rabbits hopping around!

If all those animals survived, the countryside would soon be knee-deep in rabbits. But many are eaten by owls, foxes, weasels, coyotes, and other predators. In this way, a large number of rabbits supports smaller numbers of predators. The balance of nature is maintained, and the total number of rabbits, hares, owls, and foxes remains roughly the same from year to year.

Words to Know

Bucks Male rabbits or hares.

Burrows Holes dug in the ground, where animals make their home.

Doe A female rabbit or hare.

Form A hollow in the grass, where hares and some rabbits make their home.

Herbivores Animals that eat mainly plants.

Hibernation A deep winter sleep.

Incisors The long, chisel-shaped upper front teeth of gnawing animals.

Kits Baby rabbits.

Leverets Baby hares.

Litter	A group of babies that are all born to a mother at one time.
Mammals	Animals that have hair on their body and nourish their young on milk.
Mating season	The time of year when a type of animal breeds.
Molars	The broad back teeth that are used for chewing and grinding food.
Predators	Animals that hunt other animals for food.
Prey	An animal eaten for food by another.
Species	The scientific word for animals of the same type that breed together.
Warren	An underground network of rabbit burrows.

Find Out More

Books

Miller, S.S. *Rabbits, Pikas, and Hares*. New York: Franklin Watts, 2002.

Trumbauer, L. *The Life Cycle of a Rabbit*. Mankato, Minnesota: Pebble Books, 2004.

Web sites

Arctic Hares
animals.nationalgeographic.com/animals/mammals/arctic-hare.html
Tons of facts about Arctic hares.

Rabbits
www.enchantedlearning.com/subjects/mammals/farm/Rabbitprintout.shtml
Information about rabbits with a picture to print and color in.

Index